Trash Mermaid:
Essays, Stories, Recollections, Rants, and Ramblings that Came to Me by the Jersey Sea

by Emma Tattenbaum-Fine
with illustrations by Heather Thiry

Cover illustration, as well as "Earning My Recycling Badge" illustration,
by Leah Rubin-Cadrain

DORRANCE
PUBLISHING CO
EST. 1920
PITTSBURGH, PENNSYLVANIA 15238

Dorrance Publishing Co
585 Alpha Drive
Suite 103
Pittsburgh, PA 15238
Visit our website at *www.dorrancebookstore.com*

ISBN: 978-1-6393-7531-8
eISBN: 978-1-6393-7526-4

Trash Mermaid:

Essays, Stories, Recollections, Rants, and Ramblings that Came to Me by the Jersey Sea

Words

In my real life I'm too slow. I'm ashamed that I'm still searching for the perfect word when a simple "hey got ur email. On it" would do. But I want people to feel love in my words. And it's just nice to have the time to really love you all with my words. Because I can.

Bored at the Beach

When you are bored at the beach.
Congratulations!
You have won Best Problem.
The sea goes in and out as golden
hour tips into LITERAL sunset.

The beauty makes you say
BEHOLD, I am Adonai, your God.
But you're also a little bored!
How can this be?!
The sea goes in and out and says
very plainly:
I am not a movie. I am not a bar.
I am not a sale rack at Ann Taylor
Petites, nor an ordinary, titillating
enticement.
I am not an email that would be quick and easy to answer
and make someone's day.
I am not a gel manicure
that will last five weeks
with low standards.

I am not clickbait
or an advertorial that's actually-so-interesting-hold-on-let-me-text-you-this.
I am not a steak with whipped mashed potatoes as the server comes *right toward* you.

I am not newly whitened teeth that make you less ashamed for three days.
I am not a high score, a low weight, a new Twitter follower, or a fellowship
that's really-so-hard-to-get-especially-right-now-wow-congratulations!

I'm just the infinite sea. I'll always be here, making the same old noises and
just a little boring.
I gave you crabs.
You're welcome.

Starfish at McDonald's

I was going to take care of it. That was always the plan. My tiny starfish in a Solo cup.

I smiled down at it as I carried it carefully, sloshing in its sea water, drawn freshly from the ocean, now on our way to McDonald's for a Happy Meal.

"I will take care of you" is what I told the little creature with my grasping hands, careful footsteps and wide eyes.

My parents let me keep it. And why wouldn't they? It didn't bark. It didn't bite. It took up no space.

Which toy should I get in my Happy Meal? I surveyed the options with laser focus, my head tilted all the way back to study the display case above me. I kept my starfish in its red Solo cup clutched close to my chest, resting it above my small, but promising, potbelly.

The thing with these Happy Meal toys was that you couldn't just keep getting the "Little Mermaid" over and over because that's not how you "collect them all." It was understood, among the pre-K crowd, that you *might* have to choose a non-Ariel toy sometimes, for variety's sake.

The starfish in the Solo cup made it to the table. I clambered up on my elbows to gaze in at it while I sipped my Coke. It didn't look as happy without the sand around. The inside of the cup was so smooth and empty. I wondered if it missed its friends. Ah, well, I would be its friend now!

I ate my 4-piece Chicken McNuggets in the particular way that my best friend Sarah Sommers always ate them. She ate around them in circles. It's not how I would have done it, but I wanted more to be like Sarah than I wanted to eat a McNugget in my own way.

I took out my toy: A plastic packet containing little mice characters from *Rescuers Down Under*, which was not technically a "boy movie" because Sara B. liked it. Lily H., too. It was okay to like it. And I did.

We left. My favorite place to sleep, even today, is in the backseat of the car as my parents drive.

I jerked awake in my car seat.

Where was my baby starfish?!

Sipping coffee in the driver seat at sunset, Mommy Margie says, as if she's reading the very last bedtime story, "Oh, no, did you leave it at McDonald's?"

" … …? ! ????!!!!!!

It was UNTHINKABLE.

The starfish was SO SMALL and the Solo cup SO BIG and who would see it and realize it was mine and alive and a treasure?

First, I felt the personal loss, but then I felt the murder. I should have left it in the ocean! I tried in vain to think of scenarios in which the starfish would be rescued.

I should never have taken a baby away from its home, especially if I was not even going to be its mother. It was a terrible awakening.

And what had been the plan even if I did get it home?

My moms both comforted me by explaining that it would have died anyway.

WELL, THAT WAS NOT THE GOAL.

WHAT A HORRIFIC MISCOMMUNICATION.

When my creative faculties returned to me, I chose to imagine a friendly child coming by with her fries, seeing my pet, and taking it home to her saltwater aquarium that was exactly the correct PH level to sustain a lonesome baby starfish from Jones Beach.

And.

That is exactly what happened.

The starfish is big now, thriving. Great job, beautiful family. I have no regrets. The end.

Whitefish Sandwich

Leaving Brooklyn means meeting someone nice who will say something vaguely anti-Semitic until you wade out bravely to stop them and say, before decency implodes, "I am Jewish."

Then you both sit with that.

You make a joke-adjacent statement: "I have to be Ambassador to the Jews because everyone always wants to kill us."

He laughs. Like, a little too much, actually.

And I place my stamp on the conversation:
"Now you know me. You like me. I am Jewish."

It's a good thing I'm so fucking charming.

The Odyssey: In My Own Words

CALYPSO: Odysseus, I'm *so much hotter* than your wife. Just stay on this island forever, and let's be immortal together. I can totally arrange it.

ODYSSEUS: There is *no question* that you are hotter than my wife, in large part because you have immortality, eternal youth, and sick, sick braids. However, I can't stay here as a sex slave, especially now that Hermes has flown over the ocean and said I have a shot at getting home.

CALYPSO: We've been shagging consensually and enthusiastically for seven years, and I've been cooking for you. Also I'm a goddess. Was none of that, like, a thing for you?

ODYSSEUS: Oh, yeah, no. Sorry if I led you on! Speaking of which, do you have any indestructible fabric you could turn into magical clothes for me?

(Beat.)

CALYPSO: Yeah.

ODYSSEUS: Cool, I figured.

CALYPSO: Look, I'm having a rough time with this. Wanna F once more in my sweet, sweet cave-bedroom before we spend four days building your shitty raft that's obviously gonna capsize?

ODYSSEUS: Yeah, I could get into that. For old time's sake.

The Heroine

I'm in week two of a memoir-writing workshop filled with strangers and I've written a piece, a true story, about a rather funny situation involving a horrible, terrible urinary tract infection, a hotel, a casual love affair, and some inscrutably labeled "massage lotion."

My vagina figures prominently in the story. She's the star. Not because I'm trying to make a political statement, but because ... if *you* had misused an improperly labeled massage lotion, thinking it was personal lubricant, your vagina would, unfortunately, also be the star. She will steal the show, your show, any show.

A poisoned vagina on fire will always be the star.

There is a man in this writing workshop classroom who has had it out for me since day one. I do not know why. It is exceedingly rare for people to "have it out for me." This is the first time, to date, that I've ever even used the expression.

He uses the next writing prompt of the day to write and then share a diatribe about having to "hear about this girl's vagina." He is disgusted. Afraid and therefore angry. He dedicates *his* writing assignment that day, to writing about *my* writing assignment that I've shared earlier.

This is not typical writing class behavior. A memoir class typically dwells in a space of the past and *not* in arguing with other writers in real time. He has effectively turned the classroom into a brick-and-mortar comment section.

The experience is totally mortifying. I take his "feedback," however toxically delivered, as truth.

Oh, God. He's right. How embarrassing. How could I write this true thing? This story about poisoning myself in a hotel room with a "lube" that was not actually a lube at all. No one wants this. What I had seen as bawdy and brave now feels to me a grave mistake. I must be the only one with silly vagina stories. My face flushes and my breath stays shallow.

The other 15 or so adult students sit silently. Having heard my story.

Having heard his diatribe, disguised as an assignment.

Their eyes move to our teacher, who now plays referee for what has unexpectedly turned into a tennis match of who gets to write about their privates and who does *not*.

My teacher, older than me, wiser than me, a better writer than me, is unmoved. She sits very straight and still, her jaw clenched and tells the man, with her light Scottish accent, "Maybe, you were not the intended audience for this piece."

The man is astonished.

I am astonished.

The class exhales with the surprise verdict.

Eureka! It's true! I didn't write the story for *him*. It was a story for ... if I had thought about it, really ... a story to make other vagina-owners laugh.

He leaves at the break and does not return to class again and there are still so many sessions left, and for weeks to come.

I wonder if he got a refund or if my vagina robbed him of his money and his education.

He was actually a very good writer.

Manifest

I live in a tote bag.
This. Was always the dream.
What will I do next?
Gonna see a career coach.

Art that isn't the way *I* would have done it

I see art all the time that isn't how *I* would have done it.

But.

I didn't.

Do it.

So. 😬

PUG

I saw two pugs on the beach. They were twins. I assume. They wore matching life jackets, which is *exactly* what twins would do.

Their owner was fit. Like a ballerina. The kind of ballerina who puts her twin pugs in matching green fluorescent life jackets.

😊 You know the type.

She tossed a tennis ball and the twin pugs went wild.

Well, one did.

One pug I named Speed Pug. The other, I named Slow Pug.

Can you guess why? Don't guess! I will tell you.

Speed Pug took off after the ball with a maniacal drive that came from within. Slow Pug, also happy to be there, jogged after the ball jauntily.

Were it not for the tremendous alacrity of Speed Pug, you would think Slow Pug not slow at all. You'd just call him, Pug.

But Speed Pug made a mockery of Slow Pug's performance. I hasten to add that the pugs were identical in age and size, socioeconomic background and education level. Both had an attentive, and very hot, mother.

But Speed Pug was driven from within and Slow Pug was driven by … treats?

Slow Pug, I had the sense, was just running around because that's what his family did.

But it was a very happy trio. I want you to know, because you didn't see these pugs and I did, and I feel a great responsibility to bring this account back to you: The pugs were not competitive with one another.

Slow Pug was born to follow. 🐾

His perfect destiny. 🐚 He was not ashamed. 🐾

In Ventnor City I am Lindsey-Becky-Lil Bit sitting with Shay, Big Niece, Little Niece, Phoenix and other Women whose Real Names I Never Learned

"Lindsey! Get over here."

Not my name, but I'll answer to it. I'm a tourist in Ventnor City and maybe, here, I am Lindsey and I just don't know it yet?

I leave my lonesome picnic bench and approach the table of five women.

The owner of the voice who called out "Lindsey!" offers me a shot of vodka.

I look around the otherwise quiet table and take the temperature.

I don't want to crash a circle of cozy friends who have maybe planned out this perfect night with a thousand text messages.

The table (and the vodka) has a magnetism. Donnie Darko-style, my stomach pulls me to sit. I consider the shot. "Are we the only ones drinking, though?"

No one else at the table speaks.

"Who cares what people think?!" shouts the same jubilant stranger. Big blue earrings. Blunt bangs to complement her candor.

I take the shot from her, hold it ceremoniously, and smile shyly.

My fiancé also says this to me, all the time: "Do you really care what other people think?"

Of course I do. What a stupid question. But it's the kind of question that exposes and unlocks.

We tilt the shots back, just us. Her friends look at us and maybe look down at their seafood. I'm not so aware of them. I'm really just following directions.

I can see from her outsize energy that Blunt Bangs plays the same role for her friends that I do for mine. I know that signature fatigue of the "authenticity muse" and I will surely drink with her tonight.

Now that I'm seated, questions rain down from Blunt Bangs:

"What are you, a writer, an actress or something?"

I'm flattered, delighted, embarrassed that she knew. I haven't even done my hair. I'm still not sure that the group wants me here, but the energy begins to soften and yield to Blunt Bangs, who is fully in charge of all of us.

"Where are your people from?" she asks.

"Did you see the looting in New York?"

"Do you like coffee?"

I wake up every day dreaming of coffee. She knows me so quickly.

"Come to my coffee shop," she says. "I'm gonna take you to the Black part of town."

I'm a lightweight and I become my best self so quickly, with Blunt Bangs' blessing. The silliest, the realest. It's Tourist Emma. She comes out in Israel, in Paris, and New Jersey alike. She is like a male peacock. Her feathers are beautiful, but cost a lot of energy to maintain.

Shay, the stranger formerly known as Blunt Bangs, says, "Take your hair down for the group photo."

So I do.

"Come here, Lil Bit," says Big Niece. I've learned only nicknames and I've already acquired one myself, besides Lindsey, which was temporary.

Big Niece pulls me in playfully for the photo. Her towering body, 6'1" to my 4' 10 ¾", boasts cheekbones that catch the streetlight above our picnic table. Big Niece has a stillness to her that I, as a jumpy little dog of a person, read as status. She laughs easily and I want to be the one who causes it.

She's been all night laid back so far in her chair to make room for her long torso and longer legs. Privately she tells me that these gals all met playing basketball in college.

"But you were the best?" I lean toward her, conspiratory and knowing. I was a ballet dancer and the best dancers sat like her. Their bodies radiating athletic aplomb and ease. She tosses her head playfully to say "yes," but so small a toss as to be only a tic. I sense that her gifts have caused friction among this very circle of friends. I make mental notes of who she is in *my* social circle, so that I can know her faster.

And as my drunk blonde hair swings down and we all clutch in for the photo:

"Ooh, *now* she's Becky!" shouts Shay. We all respond with a percussive eruption of snorts and gleeful giggles. I'm both mortified and honored to have landed another, this time iconic, nickname.

Lobster shells, cold fries, and shrimp tails pile up and there's a deeper peace now. We have full tummies and sleepy shoulders. I know these women only from tonight, but try so hard to read, in their jokes and glances, the two decades worth of stories they've shared since college. There's always drama among old friends, but they keep their cards close. I've certainly ruined the intimacy that might have been. Or maybe my presence gave an audience and dispelled tension or cancelled some sort of confrontation or intervention.

Shay has invited only more strangers since the night began. I wonder if she's trying to halt some kind of building intimacy that she dreads. Maybe this town is too small for her. Is she lonely? Am I?

Shay proclaims, "The police won't bug us now, we have enough white people!" Some cute Jewish boys from Manhattan have since joined us. One is a doctor and I shout, "I have antibodies!" in case he needs my plasma. (They came over in a hurry and bought us all drinks. Kept my plasma to myself, though, in spite of puppy-dog eye contact that begged me to share some.)

Little Niece is a police sergeant. She doesn't like the jokes so much. She tightens her sneaker laces and has roll call early in the morning.

Shay hollers after Little Niece about how big her butt has gotten recently. Little Niece agrees wearily with no argument and she leaves us, with a flourish of her hips performed just for Shay.

I've been told my butt was big before. By "friends" and, once, horrifyingly, by a kid I babysat. I did not take the news with a flourish of my hip, but rather with the death chortle of my soul.

If I were to move to a new town and suddenly have all new friends, I think I'd be good at this, filling in for all the lost time with my excellent memory for inane details. New friends could become old friends with just a little observation and memorization.

Big Niece asks me if I'm safe to walk home. I mark through my three standard self-defense moves that are performance ready. She is satisfied with this.

Twelve blocks away, I tumble into my Airbnb bed, still covered in a sand-sunscreen shellac from my day at the beach. I am vodka and sand and a new friend even to myself.

In Ventnor City, New Jersey, you can be anyone Shay says you are.

Hungry Wonder Woman

I look so good in my Wonder Woman bikini when I'm very hungry. After a burrito, though, I *feel* powerful, but I no longer *look* like Wonder Woman. I look like a sea lion in a lady's costume.

Ironic that when I'm hungry I *look* as though I could stop a speeding train and rescue the town. But, in practice, I would truly need that burrito first if I were going to do that.

Perhaps this is why women's empowerment is slow going.

Or maybe everybody got empowered already?!
While I was standing here, at this mirror?

Did I get left behind?
The last disempowered woman?

🏃 🏃 🏃 …….. ….. ………… ….. 🏃

Anthem of a Pioneeress

The brief respite when I charge my phone at the bar.
Leave it with a maternal bartender, mother to her own iPhone X.
She knows how to care for my baby phone.

The moment when I have a Bulleit Manhattan on the rocks in my right hand.
I have a sweet candy cherry stem in my left, yes, but
I do not.
In any hand.
Have. A. Phone.

Lo! Freedom!

I'm buzzed and without my phone.
It rests ten feet yonder, but I cannot see it and,
if it cries,
I will not come.

O! The pleasure!

Rolling hills of bourbon's grain.
Purple mountains!
Alone and a stranger in this Brave New Phone-Free Land.

This freedom is why my grandfather came to America
(also cuz Poland had no food), but definitely this! Too!

Were that my phone would *never charge* and I could know this liberty forever!

Orange Brioche

Fitting into my wedding dress is a challenge I set before me. Like all earthly challenges, it is both stupid and profound.

It is less joy today for the hours-long joy later of English net, silk-lined, with an expensive zipper.

A zipper who says, "Ah, I see. You knew the secret password. Welcome to the club," and hurries me, furtively, inside.

Warrior Woman Plans My COVID Wedding

"I am in the middle of testing shields and straws"
is the text message I receive.
The test?

A SUCCESS.

Bozrah Fairytale

I planned a weekend getaway for us near the ocean.

I am not a driver. I have my license, but I'm loath to use it. However, I wanted to be a grownup on a grownup trip with my grownup boyfriend, so I decided to borrow my parents' car and drive it to Providence. That way we'd have a car for the whole weekend.

I studied the course on a zoomed-in printed map ahead of time and I set the GPS so that Siri would scream directions at me as I drove.

(I'm also bad with geography. And just … objects that interact spatially.)

I took our Airbnb host at his word. I didn't know then that, in fact, this Airbnb was nowhere near an ocean, but rather near a small murky dock where geese came to poop and other misguided lovers came to sit, having been told there would be an ocean. If I had been better with maps, and a little less trusting, I'd have known this right away.

The whole romantic adventure seemed like a great way to incentivize driving for my frightened self:

Put some champagne in a cooler in the trunk. Place my lover at the end of the obstacle course, waiting for me in our Providence Airbnb, ostensibly, right near the ocean.

There were red flags, however, regarding the car. It was a silver Honda bought when I was halfway through high school. Used even at the time of purchase, it was now approaching its 19th birthday. My mother, Margie, though not a hoarder or miser in general, has a specific set of neuroses involving cars. Some of my earliest embarrassing memories involve her driving up to my middle school in a different Honda: A red piece of garbage so tattered and rusty that kids would point at it. On the back, it sported a gay pride flag bumper sticker.

The car was humiliating, both for me and for gay rights as a movement. My mother staunchly defended the rolling trash heap, saying that Hondas were very good cars, very safe, and that looks could be deceiving with regard to functionality. Looks were indeed deceiving, as I was always surprised when it started.

Now that the current-day, metallic-colored Honda was nearly old enough to drink, I began to have flashbacks to that red car. As it aged, the red Honda had been relegated only to short drives, deemed unworthy and uncomfortable by my other mother, Rae, who persuasively insisted that it could not handle the highway.

Margie's silver Honda was known to break down during drives in our neighborhood, however, notably, only when *I* was driving it. So Margie dismissed it as something *I* was doing. Rae would yell at her that it just wasn't a safe car, but Margie, who has a healthy and moderate relationship with every other consumer good, would always find reasons why the decrepit car could yet go on:

"It's just the position of the gas tank."

"It's just the heat."

"It's just the windshield."

As I prepared to leave, Margie insisted the car was safe and that I had nothing to worry about. A part of me knew that was illogical and that the car, in the summer heat, would misbehave to the fullest, but Margie is a born leader and has almost always been right my whole life. She is a mother that my friends have come to for sanity when their own parents failed them and I, though a full 29 years old at the time, could not fathom a scenario in which she could truly be wrong.

I began my turn onto I-84 and terror overtook me. I saw myself from the outside, hurtling forward in a few tons of combustible steel, with only my faulty instincts and high school driver's ed. to guide me. The air conditioner was busted, of course, and as my stress level rose, so too did my temperature. With the windows open and the air rushing through, I could barely hear Siri's directions, even at full volume, so I had to close the windows most of the way. The car was now a terrarium and I was baking, condensation forming all around me in the humidity of my fear, my sweat and, most pungently, my fear-sweat.

Then, 45 minutes through a 90-minute ride, the car stopped. I had about 10 seconds of lead time to note that all my fears of driving were to be validated. I was pressing the gas, everyone around me going 85 in a 75 zone, and I, a scared driver just trying to be a grownup on the way to my lover in our rented home near the ocean, began to pull myself, at 3 miles per hour, foot heavy and useless on the gas pedal, off onto the grass near the side of the zipping multi-lane highway.

I had made it halfway across the final lane when the car fully stopped. It responded to nothing. Not my heavy foot, not my steering wheel, not my string of oaths directed at my mother, who was foremost in my mind at this moment.

I put the emergency blinkers on and undid my seatbelt with great trepidation. My mind's eye whirred with vivid images of my face hitting the steering wheel as another car rear-ended me at 85 miles per hour. Everyone was speeding. I clung to my phone with my sweaty clenched claw as I scooted my butt over the passenger seat, leaving a snail trail of booty perspiration as I went, and opened the door toward safety on the grass.

Once outside the death-trap car, I relaxed enough to notice that I had to pee. My skirt and T-shirt clung to me in terror and my underwear was all bundled up in every gathering place. I called my mothers, manic and crazed. I described the situation to Rae, who, commiserating and furious, handed the phone to Margie.

I was so relieved to not be driving anymore.

Waiting for AAA I found myself hoping a car would hit the Honda, as it lay draped diagonally across the lanes like an obnoxious cat sunning itself. It was shameful how it took up so much space. Flagrantly, it defied transportation civility. A classically mortifying Margie-Honda to the very last.

I waited alone by the side of the highway in a sexy outfit that I had planned for my boyfriend, but which could now be appreciated by the entire highway. Night began to fall on the town where I was marooned, which bore the magisterial name of Bozrah.

I was increasingly uncomfortable, too, because I had ruled out peeing. If I peed, I reasoned, then I'd not only be alone by the side of the road, in a sexy outfit, but also with a bare posterior. I texted my boyfriend periodically to keep him apprised of the unfolding catastrophe. 35 minutes later, as darkness and mosquitoes brought their finishing touches to the humid evening, I saw, across the interstate, my moms and my aunt honking and waving at me, going in the other direction, some 5 lanes away. Moments later AAA pulled up, my family several minutes behind them.

Margie pulled herself out of the car, put her arm around my shoulders and walked with me alone, far from the others as they went to speak with the AAA guy. I had never seen my mother exactly like this. She reminded me of a dog who has been kicked repeatedly and then given the gift of speech. Her head was actually hung and her tailbone tucked as I felt the heavy, tired weight of her arm across my shoulder.

"I am so sorry," she said. I had never heard her so contrite. I was meeting a new side of her after all these years.

"Yeah, you messed up really, really bad!" I laughed at the sheer surprise of finding us in a situation like this: My really rather perfect mother, so out of character, making a mistake! Blinded by her weird thing about Hondas.

"What is it with you and Hondas?"

"I don't know," she admitted. "I have a real problem. I would never put you in harm's way. But then I did."

The Honda was surveyed by the AAA guy. He instantly spotted the morass of intractable existential challenges that had faced the Honda for many years. He quoted the exorbitant cost of fixing them all.

With the prognosis dire, we emptied the trunk together, removing several summers' worth of lawn chairs, towels, magazines, and of course the cooler of champagne, which I planned, now more than ever, to bring to my lover. He had long since checked in at our Providence Airbnb, using reliable public transportation to get there.

We watched as the empty Honda was dragged off to the junkyard. Moments after I had driven it, baking and reeking in fear-sweat, it was to be compacted and melted down for the next phase of its alchemical journey.

I sat in the backseat as my moms and my aunt chauffeured me the rest of the way to Providence. Each of us with our own thoughts. Margie doing some reckoning with herself. Rae doing some reckoning with Margie. Me, relieved to be in an air-conditioned vehicle, and my aunt just content to be hanging out with my colorful little family.

Later that evening I sat with Luke in a quiet rented house on a pair of stools at a marble counter. I pulled two small Korbel champagnes from the fridge, untwisted the metal around them, and he popped the corks for us. He sat in a sleeveless, loose, gray tank top, gazing at me with his kind gray blue eyes. We toasted to being together, to being alive, and took that first sip with our eyes locked.

The bubble of the crisp champagne. Safe with my prize, near the ocean (I still didn't know that I was not near the ocean). I felt like the heroine of my own fairytale.

My mother, finally having stepped down from the absurd pedestal I'd placed her on, and my own, pathetically late, but better than never, coming of age.

The ocean wasn't all that far away, but we'd have needed a car to drive to it.

Instead we sipped martinis, smoked a cigar, wandered Providence by foot, drank great coffee and fell more deeply in love. The same instincts I had about the Honda were the ones that led me to this wonderful man. My intuition was, actually, rather sharp, I thought. I would not ignore it anymore.

The Odyssey: In My Own Words (Part 2)

CIRCE: Sleep with me. I'm a witch-goddess.

ODYSSEUS: Yeah. I like your singing voice. Listen—

CIRCE: I knew it.

ODYSSEUS: I haven't said anything.

CIRCE: I knew you'd bring it up.

ODYSSEUS: You turned my men into pigs!

CIRCE: Are you mad?

ODYSSEUS: Yeah, I'm mad! And I have a hard time getting it up knowing that half my crewmen have been turned into livestock.

CIRCE: Do you, though? Have a hard time—

ODYSSEUS: No, I'm actually … pretty turned on right now.

CIRCE: Mmmkay, let's F in my goddess-witch bed and sort out the pig thing later.

ODYSSEUS: OK, *but*, for the record, when you feed me afterward, I'm gonna be pretty stressed and unable to eat.

(Beat.)

CIRCE: Will you, though?

ODYSSEUS: No, I'll probably be pretty hungry.

"FranandIrwin@earthlink.net"

The way older couples use the same email address? Discuss.

Ok, I'll go.
Every lover should have their own email address.
And I quoth, "Fill each other's cup but drink not from one cup."

I want to contact one parent and not the other. But Verizon, too, cannot distinguish them, and a text to one will go to the other. (????)

And here I quoth, "Give one another of your bread but eat not from the same loaf."

I can only understand love so much. They've been together 42 years and us just 5.

But here again, I'll add:
"Even as the strings of the lute are alone though they quiver with the same music."

And can you believe this? They actually *have* two separate and distinct addresses, but opt to use one, clarifying at the end of the email which of the lovers has penned it.
Like how Hillary Clinton will sign her own true tweets with "-H," so you can know it is *truly she* and not a staffer.

Must be dear to hold your lover so possessively and your technology so wantonly.

Russia. Wow.

That app that turned your face old ... but was actually so that Russia could steal your secrets...
has there ever been something so sci-fi?

The app *appears* to age you decades into the future. Your face is sagged and your chest heavy with memories of a life well-lived.

But what the app is ACTUALLY doing:
stealing your secrets, your identity.

Russia! Wow.
What a bottomless darkness you are.

Tools

The day you learn ... that a thing you've been doing wrong with technology—
you don't have to do anymore?

An angel gets its wings.
And so it was when I said, Mom:
Highlight it. Command C.

Now what, she said?

Command V.

Why "V" to paste?

What am I, Bill Gates? Don't know. Just do it.

She does it. Deliberately placing her small fingers like she's learning a new
chord on the piano.

Look! You just copied and pasted without using the ... dropdown ... menu thing.

Oh, yeah. Look at that. She sits back in muted wonder.

And when she goes to do it the slow way again, I stop her.
Highlight! I yell urgently, my arm flying out to shield her from oblivion.

She places one little pinky. A hair faster this time.
Now Command C!

Oh, yeah!

She places the chord again and a new chapter begins for us. I'm raising my
boomer. Giving her the tools she'll need to be a better old person on the days
when I am not, and cannot be, right beside her.

Schooner than Later

It's just a title I like. For a piece I cannot, and have no need to, write.

January Earthquake: 2020 Begins

You may recall that Puerto Rico had terrible earthquakes last January. Luke and I and my parents were staying one hour away by car from the epicenter, where there was pervasive devastation, houses split down the middle.

I felt tiny tremors a few times while at the dining room table, which I had converted into a grand desk, the base of my freelance operations. From my post I was the only one who experienced the foreboding, yet barely perceptible, shakes, but I felt in my bones that a bigger one was coming.

So I was not surprised when, in the middle of the night, our bedroom erupted with tremors. The bed rocked like we were on a houseboat in choppy water and the mirror clapped against the wall like a dying trout. Luke grabbed my arm and gripped it, more tense than I've ever seen him, and I must tell you that, while I had never experienced any immersive violence like this before, I was completely calm.

More peaceful than ever. I felt a spectacular powerlessness. I didn't feel God, I felt something far more infinite. I felt Science. And in her all things and no things are possible. I felt totally taken care of amid the rocking and shuddering of the floor and furniture. I saw, and felt, that all forms of "control" are a mirage.

When I meditate, I return to that earthquake because the sensory memory of it is the quickest way to recapture what is true.

Sometimes anxious people feel the deepest peace in crisis. Maybe how I felt in that earthquake is how other people feel when they watch reruns of *Parks and Rec.* 📺

Here Goes

When I was a very little kid (in Manhattan) and a grownup took my hand to cross the street, I thought that the philosophy behind the hand-holding was that, if a car hit us, we would die together.

I didn't know that part of being a grownup was knowing, with near certainty, that you could cross the busy street in such a way that you would, almost definitely, live.

I thought that was why grownups said, "Hold my hand," with hurried urgency, before crossing the street. You had to grab the grownup's hand quickly to ensure that, living or dying, you would do it TOGETHER.

I was never afraid to cross the street holding a grownup's hand. I thought: IF this works out like last time, we will go on living.

But every time I walked off the curb I saw that we were in total freefall with no control and any possible outcome. It wasn't even exciting. It was just true. We might die, and it's OK.

If You're Present

If you're present while eating an orange
It's splendid, actually.
The fibers and veins and slow separations are sensuous.

If you're not present
It's a punishment of boredom.

Something precious you lost in a bad trade
A school lunch fail
Poor substitute for Dunkaroos

Drops to the bottom of your backpack,
joins an old rock and a rolled-up sticker

But the trouble then is you weren't a grownup.
An orange was always this good.

Before Prozac

Before Prozac random objects made me sad. This one shirt. That one pen. That candle there. The associations were murky: Life moments coded in possessions that filled me with melancholy, which hovered like a fart cloud.

And stories always accompanied the sadness.

The shirt from the TV writing festival. Well, it *made* me sad because I didn't win some prize there or even place. The pen made me sad because I bought it at Staples on a day when I thought Staples would make me happier, but it wouldn't.

The candle had no fragrance and I bought it at a hardware store run by an addict. It was purple, but still sad.

But now they are just things.

They have gained a glow of neutrality.

A shirt is for wearing.
A pen is for a list of what needs doing by Friday.
A candle is for lighting.

Their stories have evaporated.

They were always just objects.
And, separately, a sadness in search of a narrative.

That is what Beautiful Dr. Lauren's mighty 10 milligrams can do.

Mood Swings

I was texting while the earth was tilting.
6:10 I wake up with melancholy
Turn sideways to make the sunrise my view
It thaws me and I breathe deeper.
Powerful stillness and peace suffuse me
until I can't bear it anymore
and I have to
check my phone.
It's Leah, yay. She is melancholy, stillness, and sunrise exactly and her timing
is perfect, tho she's texted hours ago.
I am deep in composing a reply about what we are learning on our parallel
journeys. Feeling wise. Feeling useful.
I look up and the sun has risen.
Kinda sad again.
To miss it.
That I couldn't bear to
just
see it.
But then I realize that this, too, is a poem.

Earning My Recycling Badge

I learned about pollution and the first vague whispers of global warming at about the same time that I grew my first pube. I was eight years old.

Precious fresh water, I learned, though it flowed limitlessly from our faucets at home, was scarce on this planet of ours.

"Have you ever been swimming in the ocean and gotten a gulp full of seawater?" my mom, Margie, asked us Girl Scouts sitting in a semicircle around her as she lectured us for our Recycling Badge. Her eyes were wide with a natural teaching instinct and a love of science. "Well," she continued conspiratorially, "most of the planet's water is like that. We are surrounded by oceans and they are *very salty*! There's only 1% of this stuff on the planet, fresh water, that we can actually drink."

The child mind is a hairy place. Ideas and fears, folktales, pop culture, religious imagery, things you learned from your mom who was leader of the Brownie troop, all form one information soup in the mind of an eight-year-old. When you're learning every day, when your mind is expanding like the universe, it is just as unpredictable and combustible as outer space.

My mother spun the globe for us Brownies, her finger sinking with terrifying emphasis into the middle of the Atlantic Ocean, "None of this is drinkable. So the water that comes out of our faucets, the water that comes from our reservoir: is very special. We have to protect it."

An absurd dialogue began to form in my malleable subconscious between the destruction of the earth at the hands of humanity, and my body's destruction at the hands of puberty.

The earth was dying and it was partly my fault for consuming resources. Resources like Lunchables, Styrofoam hot cocoa cups, My Little Pony packaging. I was growing breasts and it was partly my fault for consuming resources. Two topical issues. Two things I could not stop.

Brushing my teeth became a psychotic endeavor. I would wet the toothbrush and rapidly turn off the faucet to keep from further killing the earth by wasting water. The sound I made brushing my teeth, which could be heard through the pipes of the whole house was like this: Shhhp…… Shhhp… . Shp…shhhhhhppppp…. Shp.

At the time, my terror of hurting the planet by wasting water was joined by a more conventional childhood fear, that of *ghosts*. This new dark force I felt surrounding me like an odorless cloud, like carbon monoxide, we will come to call this as yet unnamed poison: "Fear of Puberty." But as an eight-year-old, I called it "Fear of … 🔒 … Ghosts"?

I went to my other mother, Rae, to discuss the unpleasant development of our house being suddenly haunted because I figured she'd know what to do. Unlike Margie, who was a science nerd and led the Girl Scouts toward their Recycling Badge, Rae was a shaman(!), who led the Girl Scouts toward finding their power animal. We had an incredibly progressive Girl Scout troop and often learned cool stuff for which there simply was no badge.

"I wasted water while brushing my teeth and now Grandma Beatrice is upset and she's haunting my bedroom," I told Rae as she flossed with her Waterpik.

It's my hope that when *my* child comes to me with a problem such as this … that she has "wasted" water from the faucet, a faucet connected to a suburban reservoir with plentiful water, and that a dead grandmother whom she has never met is angry at her and now haunts her bedroom … it's my hope that I'll respond, "Hmm, is there *anything else* that's maybe bothering you?"

Instead, Rae said, with her hallmark brew of competence and compassion, "Don't worry. We'll hold a séance."

Having a plan of action, I already felt better, but now of course my fears, by not being truly addressed, were validated. *Yes, wasting water was bad*, I reasoned. *Yes, one could reasonably expect to get haunted by one's grandmother's ghost if one was gonna harm the planet like that.*

The haunting from Grandma Beatrice had indeed been terrifying. The night she appeared to me, it was as she looked in her wedding photo, except naked and dancing, a young, full-grown woman, with pubic hair and breasts— similar to the new ones growing out of my body. This visit sent me running and screaming to my mothers' bedroom, attempting to explain myself.

Ghosts. Puberty. The earth dying. In defense of the grownups in my life— who would ever think that they needed to explain that these things were *un*related?

The séance began. "Beatrice," Rae intoned with her best mid-Atlantic Royal Shakespeare Company dialect, swatting burning sage up toward the ceiling. "Beatrice, Emma loves you very much and is sorry she never got to meet you, but she needs you to pass on now. It's just *too scary* to have you visit. We love you and you are free now ... to go."

"Good," I side coached softly. "That was good ... um, also though, tell her ... that I'm sorry for wasting water."

"Beatrice," Rae's classical voice rose with a cloud of sage, "Emma is sorry for wasting water."

And, as if I were Catholic, that admission and apology, sent up to Ghost Grandma Beatrice by a third party, my mother, Rae, to my mind a professional shaman, absolved me of my sins. A great heaviness leapt off my chest.

The evening's ritual now successfully completed, Rae packed up her sage and the Dixie cup she kept it in, the tools of her trade.

I was left alone in my room to explore the new silence. Sure enough, the ghost was gone.

In the vacancy, my little changing body and troubled spirit loomed larger.

Lycra Pants with a Seam

It's so mean that we gave "camel toe" a name. What might have simply been "This is how my labia express themselves in these pants" became something named and nasty.

Robbed of what is hole-y.

Camel toe is a hard thing not to have! And the time spent worrying about it in your "one wild and precious life" is time in which you had no fun at all.

In exchange for your worry, all you get is more

and ever more

camel toe.

For me, in my life, I say: Better to have had camel toe than to have had no vagina at all. ✌

Hook

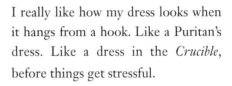

I really like how my dress looks when it hangs from a hook. Like a Puritan's dress. Like a dress in the *Crucible*, before things get stressful.

Like a catalogue of a place no one really lives.
Except that I do live here. I wear this empty black sundress that hangs so still.

And a silk (rayon/polyester) robe that hangs next to it.
I wear this in repose.
I am fancy.

Catalogues are selling what I already have.

Punch drunk in love with, and alone with, myself, over crab ravioli and good beer

The conversation is spectacular. The banter. The repartee. The depth of the questions asked and answered. The unholy truths revealed. The obscenity/the preciousness. I am the most wonderful sister-confidant that I do not have.

I would invite you but.
The conversation would turn to:

"So, what do you do?"
And what do you think of what you do?
What are the sacred problems you "have" by which you define your "self"?
I have no doubt that you're interesting but.
Can you keep up with the speed of my devilish aloneness?

This is the adult table. All the seats are taken. By facets of my warp-speed imagination.

The crab ravioli itself ... is remarkably terrible! Wow!
Like really ... wow.
How is this place even open?

But I don't care.
I'm just trying to get into my pants.

Should be easy now.

I pull down my royal blue scrunchie and saltwater hair falls to my shoulders.
I smell fantastic.

I pay my tab, and myself and I leave.
This girl is everything I've been looking for.

Pierless Fish

Luke is buying his fish now from a place called Pierless Fish.
"I get my fish now from Pierless Fish."
People have called him arrogant.
Well, wouldn't you be, if *you* shopped at Pierless Fish?
Pierless Fish autocorrects to powerless fish,
and indeed they are.
For Luke
         is going to eat them.

Get in this cup, dummy, I'm trying to help you!

Nature thumbs a taunt to the big hopeless bug, trapped and frantic, in my bedroom.

I try to be a good human, to shepherd it home (out the window), but Nature teases the bug so cruelly, singing Taylor Swift: "We are never, ever, ever getting back together."

My cup falls on empty air ten times. The long bug has so many, too many, legs. It disappears into my rumpled luggage pile, finding refugee holdings in a white T-shirt.

A salty clean breeze comes through the open window to whisper defeat to the bug: "We are never, ever, ever getting back together."

....

Up All Night with a Turkish Pop Star

I was up all night with a Turkish pop star, but in the least hot way possible. We were in an immigration law office together organizing her papers to show to United States Citizenship and Immigration Services. She was in an utter panic.

"If I don't get this Visa renewed, I don't know what I'm gonna do. I cannot go back to Istanbul. I just can't. That would basically be the end of my career. I just. Everything has to be perfect. If there is one mistake in this packet, and then I get deported … I'll never forgive myself."

Because of my OCD, most of my mantras are things like "Done is better than perfect" or "Let it be easy" or "Know when things can be Good Enough."

The Turkish pop star was harshing my mantra buzz and I was getting paid, after taxes, $12 an hour.

"Well," I said, "let's just focus on getting this done and try not to worry about the future right now."

"You don't understand what it's like to be an artist," she continued, hammering a spike through my skull with her personality as I hole punched another colorful magazine reprint proclaiming in Turkish something along the lines of "10 Things Ayla Celik* Does For Fun!" and "Ayla Celik, She's Just Like Us!"

Ayla had personally translated all the Turkish press she'd received and our office had magnified her efforts, giving great detail about the readership of each magazine in terms of numbers and outreach. The entire package, the size and heft of a textbook, was all toward one end: Proving to the US government that Ayla was sufficiently and consistently awesome enough to be deemed, for another precious two years, an "alien of extraordinary ability." Artists of all stripes all over the US spend months preparing such packages just to stay in this country and make their art.

Ayla had broken a sweat now as she fretted over the color on one of the copies, her printed glossy smiling face muted in tone as the fatigued office printer ran low on red for the third time this month.

"Oh, God, this looks awful. You're going to have to go out and get more ink," she said.

Ayla was 24 to my 28. I was reminded of *A Little Princess*, when the princess hangs out with that nasty orphan kid and they're kind of equals and contemporaries except that one is fancy and the other is nasty. But then it turns out the Little Princess' parents are dead and they are both nasty. I was the nasty one and she the princess, but then again I had American citizenship, didn't I, and I didn't need a stupid packet to get it. I started feeling incrementally more jingoistic as the night wore on and she proceeded to wear me down with her, understandable, terror and her, insufferable, narcissism.

Ayla sipped her black tea even though it was 10:45 at night. She tucked her sweaty caffeinated hair behind her ear and continued talking to me as though I was an extension of herself and not a separate person at all, "Look, it's not like I just expect citizenship here. I don't. I understand why I have to do this. I *should* have to prove that I'm worthy of this Visa. That makes sense to me. I just hate how detailed you have to be. It's so scary. Like, I have this one friend, who was at Berklee with me, incredible musician, from Israel. He failed to translate one review and they slapped him with an RFE and then something went wrong with his lawyer and they missed the deadline and that was it. His US career was destroyed. That *can't* happen to me."

I knew from what I had read about Ayla in English that she was truly a fine musician and my respect for her competed with my curiosity, which competed with my rage at being there so late, which competed with my shame for having no fancy magazine press as an artist myself and all those feelings came together so I said: "I'm hungry. Are you?"

Just then the printer, which had been churning out Ayla's face and testimonials from Americans about how useful and great she was, stuttered to a halt.

"We're out of paper … in the entire office," I said. "That was the last ream. So … I'm gonna go to CVS for paper, ink, and food. I'll be back."

By the time I got to CVS, I was dizzy with hunger. I was new to this law office day job and had not yet realized that it was 100% okay to phone it in and that no one would notice when I did. In the meantime, I kept conflating this administrative job working with artists with actual art itself and would forget to eat. I got lost in a glycemic haze on the way to the printer paper and wandered instead over to the candy. What a happy accident. Snickers Bites!

I had auditioned last week for a commercial for this very snack, newly released to the market and now in my hands. I find I am more inclined to buy a thing when I've auditioned to be in the commercial for it. When you whisper commercial copy over and over to yourself in the hallway of a casting office, the copy itself becomes a little prayer and you love the product a thousand times more than if you had simply seen the commercial on TV.

I dragged the reams of paper back to Ayla, who was on death's door back at the office, poring over the packet that would decide her fate. Would she be a big fish in the little pond of Istanbul, or an itty-bitty sweaty fish here, trying to launch her pop career? I stared blankly at her, shoveling Snickers Bites into my dry mouth. The Little Princess and the orphan, or was it the orphan and the Little Princess? Oh, wait, plot twist. Both orphans. Two New York artists in their twenties, trying to make it in the big city. Who. Cares.

Anyway, Ayla got her Visa later that year and had to go through all that garbage again two years later. I wasn't there to help because I had the privilege of quitting my day job.

To do other day jobs.

Ayla Celik is not her actual name.

Favorite Thing to Do

One of my favorite things to do is to scroll through who has seen my dumb Instagram story and admire how powerful my friends are.

I realized you should know this.

Not just that you should know that I'm incredibly well-connected and have friends who run multiple industries and I could honestly probably have you killed (but I never would! Haha!)

But just picture me, contentedly scrolling your face and thinking, wow. I *know* people.

It's a private activity. — And maybe just a little gross.

But if I tell you, and you know how proud I am, of all your faces as they whiz by…

Maybe it's not so private! Now that I've told you.

I am so impressed by all of you.

Thank you for looking at whatever it was you looked at for half a second. I saw you seeing me and I'm amazed by you. 💀

The Going-Away Party

Once someone threw a going-away party in my honor because I was moving.

The mother of a child I'd babysat for a long time graciously insisted that they host a party for me and invite another family I babysat for.

I prepared for the party as if preparing to attend my own funeral.

Not only was I an old-ass babysitter, I was being celebrated as such. It was like a macabre parody of the Kennedy Center Honors. For years of achievement in babysitting. I pictured Carole King singing about me as I mopped up vomit.

Initially I was horrified at the invitation and the idea. Then, moments later, I was deeply touched.

I saw outside myself in a rare moment of clarity that I almost never had in my mid-20s. From a mother's perspective, I was not a loser. Not only had I kept these two children alive, they had perhaps come home and even babbled good and peaceful things about our time together. I could see through my bitterness long enough to perceive that it was a pure service I had provided.

The invitation forced me to be present with the idea that my time was being spent. One way or another, I had spent it—whether in denial or in full consciousness—it was now past. Placing the details of the party in my paper calendar, I mocked the celebrants with my pen strokes, "Don't you know who I am? I'm far too good for babysitting and deeply unworthy of being celebrated and…."

Which was it, though? Was I too good? Or was I not good enough?

The stories crashed and burned on one another.

Was I mortified or exalted?

Or was I a person who had done a job and was now leaving it and therefore got cake?

No matter where I looked, I was mismatched with the situation. But I *was* the situation. I was the one living it. I was two witnesses making improbable and opposite pleas to a jury. One said, Emma is above this. Another said, Emma is beneath this.

And on the "big" day. 🧜‍♀️ … 😳

Competing with both witnesses was my own account now: A party. A living room of laughing people with grateful, smiling eyes to whom I was grateful back.

I left the party with a covered-in-tinfoil paper plate, frosting peeking out the side. I sensed vaguely, in a peace that was trying desperately to reach me, "You're on your right path. All things are in place."

Under Promise and Over Deliver

When the minifridge freezes my little orange I watch amazed, amused, disappointed, annoyed as steam rises from its skin. It sits on my desk like a Cirque du Soleil spectacular. Dry ice and emotionally stunted acrobats tumbling from it like Polichinelles.

Seeing this, I want to embrace my minifridge and say,

You are enough. You have done enough. Let the freezer freeze and you! You just be a fridge! It is enough to simply be what you are.

My orange defrosts in the August morning heat. Sublimating and relieved.

Maybe I'm projecting.

Dr. Lauren, My Beautiful Italian Teladoc Muse

When Prozac has stabilized, I will tell you what it is. It is Tiger's Blood.

In the first months it was story dreams and sleep thirst. Crawling through a desert in a tantalizing drip of veil-thin sleep, seeking deep rest that never came.

But now, months in, it is engaging with a clean mania, holding her in a closed jar like a lightning bug and a dragonfly, electric roommates trapped together.

And I can hold the jar in peace while they spar for space and bang around the glass.

Not entirely pleasant,
but spectacular power.

The Big Reveal

What a lie you were sold that you are here to entertain others.
You are not.
You are here to have your hands full of garnet leaves.
Your mouth full of butternut ravioli.
Your toes full of sunset sand.
Your face baptized by doggie kisses.
Maybe, the world is the performer,
And you have been
An inattentive audience.

A Very Good Cardiologist

During a phase of hypochondria, I took myself to a cardiologist. My symptoms were a racing heart that I reasoned could be anxiety, or from running uphill in Central Park midsummer, or from I Was Dying. I wanted to rule out one of those. At Mount Sinai I met the most curious little cardiologist.

In the exam room, she listened to my heart like it was the first heart she had ever heard.

"Did you feel that?"

"Feel what?" I said.

"Your heart just skipped a beat," she said, her eyebrows lifted: "Benign heart murmur. Pretty cool."

Was this consummately professional-looking, middle-aged woman actually an intern? Shouldn't she be, I don't know, more bored by my heart? More bored by all hearts, at this point in her career?

She ordered an echocardiogram and the results showed a healthy cardiac muscle with flexible walls.

Back in her office now, the cardiologist took the opportunity of my well visit to instead discuss ... her love of comedy. ☺

She leaned over her desk and told me, "We have so many very funny things we see, but only cardiologists would really get them. So, sometimes," she smiled in private pleasure, "sometimes I imagine this gathering, like a conference of cardiologists, where we do funny skits just for one another."

I wanted her to tell me some of the hilarious cardiology jokes she was harboring, but was sobered to realize that I'd need years of medical school, a residency, and several years in private practice just to understand one joke that, in all likelihood, I'd have a lot of notes for.

I chose instead to observe her joyful, silly spirit and that did make me laugh.

As I exited, she told me that she had recently attended a Bat Mitzvah where the floor of the party room was entirely filled with sand to make it like a beach. Was that, in my experience, typical of Bat Mitzvahs?

No, I told her, that was, in fact, quite ridiculous. And she smiled again, because everything in her life was a great adventure.

Her simple, goofy gratitude was contagious.

My heart felt better.

At the End of the Day

At the end of the day I make a list of everything I've given up on.

The emails that didn't get sent.

The follow-ups to follow-ups which will not be followed up on.

The social media posts for which I'm remunerated in exchange for screaming into multiple voids. Each void with its own code of etiquette for existential preening.

And when the list is done, I die a little.

I admit that I'm not a highly effective machine, or even a creaky machine, or any machine at all.

I am small, my left foot hurts some days, and my heart skips beats that only I can hear. Sometimes I trip cuz my back is crooked and I stand too much to the left.

Careen into objects.

These falterings make me think I won't make it to 112 years old like the ladies in Italy and Japan. Or 150 years old when The Singularity comes. I'll just be too sleepy by then. I'll just give up. Pumped full of microchips and new sprung knees, but I'll—just—be—too tired. And give in. Like I do now at the end of this day.

The Odyssey: In My Own Words (Part 3)

Odysseus knocks on the corner office door.
Athena looks up from her desk.

ODYSSEUS: Hey.

ATHENA: What's up?

ODYSSEUS: Do you have a moment./

ATHENA: /Sure.

Athena puts down a sheet of graph paper covered in parabolas.

ODYSSEUS: 50 suitors is a lot for one man to kill.

ATHENA: Oh. This.

(Beat.)

ODYSSEUS: What if the bronze weapons melt? I'm also unclear on the omen re: "the dove and the eagle." Was it good?

Athena tosses her head back and rolls her eyes.

ODYSSEUS: What was your—read on that?

Athena continues to roll her head and eyes around. She's mock dying.

ODYSSEUS: I'm sorry to be weird about it. I just—50 seems like a lot.

ATHENA: Sure, but I'm a goddess.

Odysseus nods.

ATHENA: I'm also your boss.

He bites his lip.

Athena: A lot of men go into battle with, like, a friend they met at a tavern/
ODYSSEUS: /Yeah.
ATHENA: /a mortal friend who sounded brave after a few wineskins. You're going into battle with a goddess.
ODYSSEUS: You ok if I pray to Zeus too, though?/
ATHENA: /You do you.
ODYSSEUS: /Just in case.

She returns to her graph paper parabolas.
Odysseus begins to pray to Zeus.
Athena can't let it go. She looks up, annoyed.

ATHENA: I'm the goddess of "wisdom, courage, inspiration, civilization, law and justice, *strategic warfare*, mathematics, strength, strategy, the arts, crafts, and skill."*
ODYSSEUS: So awesome! (Fiddles with his toga.) But it's a lot of suitors. They're young. They're eating so much livestock. I just ...

She gives a withering stare.

ODYSSEUS: Thanks for being so ... understanding.

She writes out a string of numbers, an equal sign and a triumphant numerical answer on her graph paper.

ATHENA: (Not looking up.) You have toothpaste on your toga.
ODYSSEUS: Oh.

ATHENA: Close the door on your way out.

ODYSSEUS: K.

ATHENA: Lemme know when it's/

ODYSSEUS: /Bye.

ATHENA: /time to kill.
*https://greekgodsandgoddesses.net/goddesses/athena/

Heroic J Encounters the Sea

J runs toward the sea with her mouth open wide
She's ready to ride it till brine gets inside
She's briefly knocked out, not even yet started
but she's here for the day and not to be thwarted
The ocean has called her from subways and track rats
to dabble in magic of this sort and that tack
to try out her power, its methods unfolding,
to spar with her loneliness, ever embold'ning
"Not today, doubt," she remounts the board.
It is her dominion and she is its lord.
The sea claims her again, but this time it laughs.
She's drunk with exhaustion and kelp at her calf.
Expectations have shifted, J has no more pride.
The moon has whispered a scold to the tide.
And now all lies quiet for J's very first ride.
Sensing her moment, she clambers on board.
It is her steed. She holds forward her sword.
She rides into a wave—it's a monster uncaring
but in tune with its roar she is ever more daring!
It crests over her now, she is lifted and falling.
Held in suspension, to surf is her calling!

The Post-Brunch Selfie

I'm not thirsty—I'm not hungry—I don't hafta pee.
I'm not too hot. I'm not too cold.
I'm not injured. I'm not even sad.
I am on the beach. I am *reading poetry.* (!!! 😊) In an un-ironic way!
Today I am the point one of the point one of the "one peh-cent." (-Bernie 🧤🧤)
My only complaint right now, if I had one, is that I'd like Quiet(!), but I
can't. stop. thinking. up. *my own* poems.

Upon completion of this voyage, Special Thanks is due to:

Rae Tattenbaum and Margery Fine—my parents, who are fun and funny and in love

Jenna Dioguardi—for all of her editing and creative support

Elizabeth Swados, Preston Martin, Matt Gehring, Ravenna Lipchik, Ali Levin, Valerie Peterson, Leah Rubin-Cadrain, Jaclyn Backhaus, Andrew Neisler, my sister collaborators at KAL Media, Annie Tippe, James Rees, Marie Carter, Harlan Alford, Audrey Schomer, Julie Shapiro, Chessy Brady, Alyssa Reuben Sedrish, Shannon Tyo, Ariana Seigel, Janani Sreenivasan, Rita J. King, Christine Ma, and Michelle Tattenbaum—*who have all nurtured my writing at pivotal moments.*

Luke Krafka—my beloved and my cheerleader

Nick Krafka—my brother-in-law, who supplied the title, "Trash Mermaid," as we all floated in the Cape Cod sea

Mike—the most detail-oriented, kind, outstanding Airbnb host, who stocked the minifridge with healthy treats so I could write

Thank you for coming!
Tip your bartender!
Exit this way.

CPSIA information can be obtained
at www.ICGtesting.com
Printed in the USA
BVHW021129130322
631287BV00001B/1